D1415385

Inside Photography

By Annie Buckley and James Buckley, Jr.

The Child's World®
www.childsworld.com

Published in the United States of America by The Child's World®
1980 Lookout Drive • Mankato, MN 56003-1705
800-599-READ • www.childsworld.com

Extra-special thanks to the photographers who not only
let us into their worlds, but also supplied us with examples of
their wonderful work!

ACKNOWLEDGMENTS

The Child's World®: Mary Berendes, Publishing Director

Produced by Shoreline Publishing Group LLC
President / Editorial Director: James Buckley, Jr.
Designer: Tom Carling, carlingdesign.com
Cover Design: Slimfilms

Photo Credits
Cover–Mike Eliason (main and inset); Ralph Clevenger, Larissa
Underwood (insets).
Interior–20-29: © Ralph Clevenger; 12-19: Courtesy Mike Eliason/
Santa Barbara News-Press; 4-11: Courtesy © Larissa Underwood .

Copyright © 2008 by The Child's World®
All rights reserved. No part of this book may be reproduced or
utilized in any form or by any means without written permission
from the publisher.

LIBRARY OF CONGRESS CATALOG-IN-PUBLICATION DATA

Buckley, Annie.
 Inside photography / by Annie Buckley and James Buckley, Jr.
   p. cm. — (Reading rocks!)
 Includes index.
 ISBN-13: 978-1-59296-867-1 (library bound : alk. paper)
 ISBN-10: 1-59296-867-8 (library bound : alk. paper)
 1. Photography—Juvenile literature. 2. Photographers—Juvenile
literature. I. Buckley, James, 1963- II. Title. III. Series.

 TR149.B76 2007
 770—dc22

                          2007004193

CONTENTS

CENTRAL ARKANSAS LIBRARY SYSTEM
ADOLPHINE FLETCHER TERRY BRANCH
LITTLE ROCK, ARKANSAS

LIFE BEHIND THE
Camera

Taking pictures is easy, right? You just point a camera at something and—click! Well, it's not always that easy. In this book, we'll meet three different photographers. As you'll learn, being a photographer takes much more than just pointing and clicking.

"I was always the one carrying the camera," Larissa Underwood says with a smile. Larissa grew up in a family of creative people. As a little girl, Larissa liked taking pictures. It wasn't until

a college photography class that she knew she wanted to be a photographer. After attending photography school, Larissa worked with other photographers in New York City. Then she started out on her own. Larissa now lives and works in Los Angeles, California, where she takes pictures of celebrities—singers, actors, models, and others.

*Larissa (inset) often sets up shots in a **studio**. Her work often makes well-known people look very beautiful.*

Larissa's Portfolio

A photographer's **portfolio** is a book of photographs that best shows the photographer's style. Larissa's portfolio has four chapters. She updates it once a year. Her portfolio includes pictures of movie stars, active people, beautiful fashions, and bands and musicians, among many other things.

Larissa loves her job. She also says that, while photographing the stars is fun, it's also a lot of work! Before she gets behind the camera, Larissa has a lot of things to do. She gathers and checks her equipment. She talks with magazine companies and **publicists** who hire her. And she works on her portfolio. Some days, she gets called to do a **photo**

shoot the next day and has to prepare quickly. Other days, she meets with her **agent**, who helps her find jobs to do. She might also meet with people who want to hire her to take photos.

Larissa posed this model with large, black tires to match the model's cool, dark clothing.

Here, a black umbrella helps direct light on Larissa's model. Knowing how light works is a big part of a photographer's work.

Before a photo shoot, Larissa finds out what her **client** is looking for in the photograph. The lighting, clothing, makeup, and **location** all affect the way the photo will look. She also helps decide what mood or feeling the client wants.

Some pictures are bright and sunny and others are moody and dark. If they decide to shoot in a studio, Larissa sets up the equipment and lighting ahead of time. When on location, Larissa might choose a beach, restaurant, or a home for the background of the photo.

Do you ever get nervous before getting your picture taken? The singers and actors Larissa photographs feel the same way! She helps them relax first. Sometimes she plays music and asks them to dance! But the most important thing Larissa does is to stay calm herself. She does a lot more than just push a button on her camera.

Here, Larissa is on location at a beach. It's beautiful, but Larissa is there to work hard! She has to understand the sunlight, and even deal with the wind.

For each photo shoot, Larissa has a team of hairstylists, makeup artists, and assistants. Larissa has a special camera that puts the photos right into a computer. That way she and her team can check right away to be sure everything looks the way they want it to look.

After a photo shoot, Larissa has hundreds of images to choose from! How does she know which is the right one? First, she looks through all of the images to select the best ones. She looks at the **expression**,

composition, and lighting. She also looks for pictures that tell a story. The clients then choose the pictures they want . . . and there's more work to do. Larissa uses a computer to adjust color and lighting to give the chosen photographs "something special." Larissa feels lucky to have a job she loves. She says, "Every day, every time I pick up the camera, I learn something new!"

Here's the result of Larissa's work on the beach. The models look great, the lighting is just right . . . and her client is happy with her work!

CAPTURING THE news

A huge fire had broken out on the wharf in Santa Barbara, California. Bright orange flames lit up the night sky. Mike Eliason rushed to the scene. He's not a firefighter, though—he's a photographer. It's the job of news photographers like Mike to be ready at a moment's notice. They take news photos that show readers what's going on in the world.

Mike knew the fire was a big story the moment he got to the wharf. "For the first time in my life, I told them to hold the presses [stop printing the paper]," Mike says. "They gave me an hour to take pictures!" Mike found a safe place and clicked away. The next morning, readers woke up to read about the fire. They saw several of Mike's amazing pictures of the towering flames.

Braving the flames, Mike took this photo of the Stearns Wharf fire in Santa Barbara.

Action-packed photography like the wharf fire is nothing new for Mike. He has been a photographer for the *Santa Barbara News-Press* for 20 years. Mike has even won state and national awards for his photographs.

Mike basically takes three kinds of photos: news, **feature**, and sports.

It's in the Bag

News photographers like Mike keep bags of equipment in their cars for any emergency. Mike has a different bag for winter (right) and summer. Each has clothing, energy bars, water, and towels, among other things. He also has bags of camera gear such as lenses, **tripods**, and lights.

Let's look at each type of photo.

Like the fire, news happens all the time. Mike listens to special radio signals to find news. When he hears something happening, he heads to the scene.

"We don't enjoy seeing people suffering, such as in a fire or at a traffic accident," Mike says. "But we have the responsibility to be there to help tell the story.

Mike carries two cameras. He uses a small camera to take close-ups. A larger one takes pictures from farther away.

"The first pictures we take cover the whole scene. Then we move in for close-ups of people and details."

Every news scene has its own challenges. At fire scenes, Mike must make sure he doesn't get in the way of firefighters or police officers. Traffic accident scenes can be on busy streets or rain-slicked highways. "We have to make sure we're aware of everything around us," he says.

On the scene: Mike captured singer Michael Jackson (under the umbrella) dancing on top of a car!

At the scene of this fallen bridge, Mike captured the feelings of a man who escaped from the car at the bottom.

Once he's on the scene, Mike looks for action or a moment that might make a great picture. But it's not as easy as just pointing and clicking. He juggles two cameras, a bag, and a notebook. He moves around trying to get the light to work the best way for the photo. And he has to do it quickly. If he misses a great photo moment, he might not get another chance. "They won't make an arrest again just so I can get a photo I missed," he laughs.

Along with news pictures, Mike also takes pictures to go along with feature stories in the newspaper.

"I approach each assignment as a puzzle, and I try to solve that puzzle," he says. "I have an idea in mind when I get to the location, but once I get there, we often have to be creative. The challenge is to make something other than the ordinary picture."

Mike also loves sports and tries

Mike has a lifelong love of flying. He took this picture of himself for a story on flying a glider.

to shoot games when he can. For sports photography, he says it's important to know the sport you're shooting. "You want to be able to guess where the action might be so you're looking at the right place."

The life of a news photographer is active and sometimes dangerous. But Mike really loves what he does. "I love the challenge of capturing real life for our readers," he says.

On feature assignments, Mike might have his subjects pose with props, such as sports gear or something that the person works with.

Taking great sports photos like this one means thinking ahead to what might happen . . . and having your camera ready to shoot!

3

PHOTOGRAPHING Animals

On a sunny day off the coast of Australia, Ralph Clevenger was enjoying an ocean swim. Dressed in full **scuba** gear, he floated just below the surface. Suddenly, from out of the depths came an enormous shark! As its jaws opened wide to turn Ralph into lunch, Ralph pulled out his underwater camera and started shooting. Good thing Ralph was in a steel cage at the time.

Ralph is an underwater and nature photographer. He takes pictures of animals above and below the water. Along the way, he's had adventures around the world. Ralph combines a childhood love of nature with years of study in photography to create some beautiful pictures.

OPPOSITE PAGE
A shark attracted by blood in the water gave Ralph this toothy smile.

Ralph tells young photographers that the best way to learn is to take pictures . . . lots of them!

Ralph didn't start out wanting to be a photographer—he trained first as a **marine biologist**. In his first job, he took underwater pictures to help scientists. He liked it so much, he decided to take photography classes. He studied at the Brooks Institute of Photography in Santa Barbara, California. "That's when I finally realized that photography could be my career," he says. "Brooks showed me how to open up my thinking to include nature, sports, adventure, travel, and more."

Ralph's main interest is the world of the sea. Being an expert scuba diver is the first step. Learning to be patient is the second!

"You're moving and the water is moving and the fish are all moving," he says. "It's a challenging environment. It's also as close to flying as you can get!"

This picture of fish moving through a kelp forest looks almost like a painting.

Coral? Yes, but there are also bright-red Christmas tree worms in this photo. Ralph's studies of undersea life help him take great pictures.

To get his pictures, Ralph usually finds a beautiful spot and lets the creatures come to him. "I could chase them around, but they're all much better swimmers than I am!"

Ralph says that knowing as much as you can about the animals you want to photograph will help you take great pictures.

Ralph used a guide to help him find and photograph this leafy sea dragon.

To photograph sharks, Ralph floats inside a steel cage. This one was just feet away from a great white!

"You should find out their habits and patterns, when they like to be out, or where they might be found," he says. That's true of both land and sea animals.

If you're looking for animals to photograph, Ralph calls the hours just around sunrise and sunset "animal time." He says that most animals are active during those hours, so that's a good time to keep your eyes peeled.

To capture this split-second action of leaping salmon, Ralph had to wait for hours!

Not all of Ralph's photos are taken when he's wet. Some are taken when he's cold! "I once spent four days in Alaska sitting on a small wooden platform. I was waiting for grizzly bears to grab the salmon swimming upstream. I got the bears' pictures, but also took some just of the salmon. I've sold more salmon pictures than bear pictures!" That's proof that you have to be ready for anything when taking pictures in the wild.

Ralph has also photographed lions and other animals in Africa, buffalo in Yellowstone National Park, and dozens of other animals, big and small.

While in Africa, Ralph caught this awesome close-up photo of a male lion.

Ralph says this spider picture combined patience, his knowledge of animals, and sticking with it.

The spider picture below taught Ralph a lot. He wanted to photograph a daddy longlegs spider against a sunset. He set up a flat rock with the sunset in the background and placed the spider on the rock. But the spider kept running under the rock. "So I stopped and thought like a spider. And I realized that he was acting normally, running away from open space. I put a small cover over the rock and got the picture!"

One more from Mike: He was in an airplane when he took this amazing picture of a helicopter fighting a forest fire.

Whether photographing beautiful models, roaring fires, or toothy sharks, all photographers share similar skills. As Ralph says, "I don't 'take' pictures, I 'make' pictures by combining what I see with what I know [about photography]." All three "shooters," as they're sometimes called,

The key to this picture by Larissa is making sure the model's face was perfectly lit.

combine camera technology with their eyes as artists.

Hours of hard work, patience, and planning go into a photograph that's captured in the blink of an eye. Without that work ahead of time, a photo might be missed, or simply not as good.

As you take pictures yourself, remember the words of these experts: Be open to new ways of seeing something. Be ready at all times to take pictures. And take *lots* of pictures. In photography, as in most things, practice will make you better . . . and, someday, perfect. In this case—picture perfect.

Ralph took a swim with sea lions to get this photograph.

GLOSSARY

agent a person who helps an artist, actor, or photographer meet people and get jobs

client a person or company that hires or buys goods or services

composition the way the elements of a photograph are arranged

expression a look on someone's face that shows thoughts or feelings

feature in newspapers, a story that is usually about a person or group who has done something interesting

location a term used to describe the place where photographs are taken away from a photo studio

marine biologist a scientist who studies animals that live in the water

photo shoot the time when a photographer takes pictures of models

portfolio a book that contains examples of a photographer's style

publicists people who work to draw attention to actors, photographers, artists, or companies

scuba a word that means gear used by divers

studio a place where an artist, photographer, or musician works

tripods poles with three legs used to support cameras

FIND OUT MORE

BOOKS

The Kids' Guide to Digital Photography
by Jenny Bidner (Lark Books, 2004)
This book helps you learn how to take better pictures with
your digital camera.

Photography (Eyewitness Books)
Dorling Kindersley, 2004
Everything from the history of photography to how cameras
work, with tons of—what else?—photographs.

Picture This: Fun Photography and Crafts
by Debra Friedman (Kids Can Press, 2006)
Do more than just put your pictures on the wall. This book
gives you more fun ways to use the pictures you take.

WEB SITES

Visit our Web page for lots of links about photography and the
photographers in this book: www.childsworld.com/links

Note to Parents, Teachers, and Librarians: We routinely check our Web links to
make sure they're safe, active sites—so encourage your readers to check them out!

INDEX

ANNIE BUCKLEY is a writer and teacher in Los Angeles. She is also an artist, and much of her work involves photography, along with other media.
JAMES BUCKLEY, JR., has written more than 40 books for young readers on a wide variety of topics. Annie and James are a brother-and-sister writing team for this book!